NOT JUST DONKEYS

Dr Elisabeth D. Svendsen M.B.E.

illustrations by Eve Bygrave

Whittet Books

First published 2008

© 2008 by Dr E. D. Svendsen, M.B.E.

Whittet Books Ltd, South House, Yatesbury Manor, Yatesbury, Wiltshire
SN11 8YE

British Library Cataloguing in publication data
A catalogue record for this book is available from the British Library
ISBN-13 978-1-873580-76-9

The Donkey Sanctuary, Sidmouth, Devon, EX10 0NU
A charity registered with the Charity Commission for England and Wales.
No. 264818
Tel: (01395) 578222
Fax: (01395) 579266
www.thedonkeysanctuary.org.uk
by the same author:

The Bumper Book of Donkeys
A Donkey Doctor's Diary
Donkey Tales
Down Among the Donkeys
For the Love of Donkeys
From Dawn to Dusk at the Donkey Sanctuary
In Defence of Donkeys
A Passion for Donkeys
Travels for a Donkey
The Tale of Naughty Mal
A Week in the Life of the Donkey Sanctuary

to Paul

My rock, without whose support
The Donkey Sanctuary would not be where it is today

Blackie and Lola: Blackie was saved from Villanueva de la Vera.

The Old Donkey

It's quiet at night in the Donkey's Barn
The silence disturbed by a rustle
As an elderly donkey slowly lies down,
Protected from life's daily bustle.

Her eyes may be dim as she lies on the straw
Outstretched, her flanks hardly moving.
Thoughts of before, filled with fear and with pain
Of a past life, which is slowly improving.

Does she sleep, as we do, through hours of the night?
Is she able to escape from her past?
Or is she forever, doomed to remember
Awake, till the dawn comes at last?

Should we, as her carers, feel guilt and remorse
That our species can be inhumane.
That cruelty comes in a daily dose
Inflicted to cause greatest pain?

This seems the right moment, as we're gathered here,
To remember those suffering today.
And just take a moment to think of them all,
And for that poor old Donkey to pray.

1
Early Days

I suppose a phone call from a Bank Trust to tell you that you have been left a legacy would be a shock, but would also bring visions of a pleasant surprise? Not so for me – that telephone call on June 20th 1974 was to cost me my husband and to change my life forever!

Born in Yorkshire in 1930, I had a lovely childhood, with loving parents and a caring sister – I also had a special friend, June Evers. We met on the first day of school in 1935 – both being dropped off from our parents' cars, and left to knock on the great big wooden door in front of us, literally scared to death! This first encounter started a relationship that is even stronger today, 72 years on.

The war was a big event in both our lives and meant we could no longer attend the same school as we lived in different towns. However, we met every weekend and June kept me company many evenings when I was so ill with septicaemia and osteomylitis. June went on to study Radiography, eventually retiring from her position as Chief Radiographer at Exeter Hospital.

When I was about 7, every third weekend my parents set off in our little Hillman Minx car – JX 1830, on the rough cobble journey to St Anne's on Sea, where my grandparents had retired to. I'm afraid I made them add an extra 10 miles to the trip, to go past a field on the way where 2 donkeys lived. Dad would stop and

I would run up the bank and shout 'donkeys' and they always came to me! I was fascinated by their beautiful eyes and soft warm muzzles and dreaded father's rather irritating 'toot toot' that told me the boring journey was about to recommence. At our destination I always refused to ride on the beach donkeys because they looked tired and thin.

As I grew older I decided to follow my sister Pat's example and trained as a teacher, obtaining a 1st Class Froebel diploma. I was very moved when we were taken to a special needs' hospital, and appalled that the children were literally tied up in cots or beds for most of the day and not given any opportunity to learn or progress.

After teaching for almost two years a crisis in the family firm persuaded me to join my father and I became secretary of a pipe works! I learnt typing and took a business course, and was soon running that side of the business. Occasionally my father asked me to call on clients and I believe I was the only lady to be travelling in drain pipes at that time!

Meeting Niels Svendsen was a turning point in my life – my car caught fire and he put it out! Six months later we were married, and a wonderful relationship started that was to last for 27 years.

Niels took a job in Bridgwater, Somerset and, with my new baby, Lise, and many regrets, I left the family firm and moved into a flat in the old manor house – Stockland Manor. The biggest disadvantage was that we were not allowed to dry nappies outside. In those

days disposable nappies were not an option, and it was 2 nappies for every change – a Harrington square and Towelling square – slow to dry! Clever Niels developed a nappy dryer, and soon we were running a thriving business – me selling them during the day and doing the business side, and Niels making them in the tool shed in the evening. By this time my second baby, Paul, was well on the way and many a time I longed to relax in the bath – but it was full of half-made dryers.

The *News Chronicle* was running a 'Get Ahead' competition with a prize of £5,000 for the best business idea – (and in those days, 1958, this was a lot of money). We won and our company was on the map!

By 1961 Clive was on the way – the business was booming and we had a big factory in Yeovil. We were approached by Thorn Industries and eventually sold out to them. Unfortunately it didn't work out too well and Niels hated being an employee – he was an 'entrepreneur'. We moved on, starting as business consultants, running and putting a shipyard on its feet in Falmouth and doing various consultancy jobs. Then Niels hurt his back and had to lie down for 6 weeks. We thought and thought and decided a change of direction was needed – to own a hotel would fit the bill – if Niels' back was too bad we would have staff to help. It sounded ideal, and for me a hotel with land and fields would allow me to have donkeys! So we bought the Salston Hotel! At first we lived in the hotel, but this was not very easy with three children! Very fortunately a lovely house became available adjoining the hotel grounds – it had a large garden, around two acres, including a large walled area, and stabling. It was just what we needed, ideal to be so close to the hotel, but with privacy to bring up the children – not to mention it proved ideal for donkeys as well.

Our first resident donkey was Naughty Face. She was so beautiful, donkey grey with the largest eyes and, unfortunately, the loudest voice I had ever known! I became accustomed to residents complaining they had been woken at 4 a.m. by this terrible noise! I couldn't think why she was so unhappy. I moved her further away from the hotel, but the cries seemed even louder. I suddenly realised she must be lonely, as she would never bray when I was with her – and so I bought Angelina – a deep chocolate mare, and peace reigned! Needing to know much more about their needs and care, I joined the Donkey Breed Society, eventually becoming a Council Member and Area Representative for the South West, and started breeding donkeys in a small way. It was at this point that my life began to change. My little stud farm was successfully breeding superb healthy donkeys, but I had not realised that all donkeys were not as well cared for as mine, and those of the Donkey Breed Society members.

A new member wanted to buy a donkey, and I was asked to look out for a suitable purchase for her. I saw some donkeys were for sale at Exeter Livestock Market and went along, never suspecting what I was going to see.

There in a pen, on the edge of the market, were seven small terrified donkeys. They were covered in lice,

their feet were long and they just looked so pathetic! I
tried to buy the one that looked worst, but the dealer
wanted £45.00 and it was obviously a lot of money, for
a donkey looking at death's door. I walked round for
a few moments, then decided I just couldn't leave that
desperate donkey and walked back to the pen – but
I was too late – along with the others, he was being
roughly herded up the ramp of a large cattle lorry, tail
twisted cruelly, and an electric cattle goad prodding him
on for good measure! Despite my pleas, and offers of
£50.00 – it was no use: 'They're going to work on a
beach, and they're all sold,' was the rough reply as the
ramp of the lorry was slammed shut. I met that donkey
3 months later – collapsed on the beach, covered with
a dirty sack, and, with my husband, we carried him
into our trailer and took him home where, after two

months of love and veterinary care, he made almost a full recovery despite having had a heart attack and being elderly.

Still searching for a suitable donkey for the Donkey Breed Society lady, I saw one offered in the local press. The owner offered to deliver it to the hotel and assured me it was in good condition. I got back from a trip to the cash and carry for the hotel and Niels told me the donkey had arrived. I tried to approach her in the field, but she was terrified and kept backing away – I thought it better to leave her until morning as there was food and water in the field. Early the next morning we were wakened by the donkeys' desperate braying. Looking out from our window we could see them all surrounding a grey shape lying on the ground. We rushed out and found her lying stretched out, unable to rise and her breathing was laboured and shallow. We thought we would need help to carry her to a stable, but to our surprise the two of us were able to lift her and carried her carefully and placed her on a deep bed of straw and covered her with a blanket. As I spooned warm milk and glucose down her throat, Niels rang the vet. He was very concerned, as she was almost starved to death and the fight for her life began. The dealer, when phoned and told in no uncertain manner what a cruel state she was in, said, 'I'm really surprised – she was the best of the lot.'

It took hours to get her eating again, and I knelt by her side, gently brushing her matted coat, which came away in lice ridden lumps – but by evening she was able to stand. My son, eyeing her solemnly, decided she could

be called 'Smartie' now and so she got her name.

I had not realised there were so many donkeys in trouble in England, so I opened my doors to those in need, and in came the donkeys – some with horrific injuries, having been beaten, teeth smashed, and for a poor little donkey called Tiny Titch, sacking embedded in his shattered spine, and those starved and ill. Some came from a Miss Philpin who had a donkey sanctuary near Reading. They would arrive in a superb horse transporter and stagger out in all stages of distress, to the obvious concern of the driver who was more used to carrying race horses.

Eventually we had 48 donkeys in care, and the cost was becoming impossible as the hotel had yet to come into profit, so we registered our South Western Donkey Sanctuary as a charity to allow us to raise funds for our donkeys.

And so we came to June 20th, 1974, and that phone call – it was Niels' birthday and we had been celebrating at the hotel and returned home shortly after 11 p.m. My son, Clive, was waiting for us: 'Mum, no matter what time it is you have to phone this telephone number in Reading – he sounds very posh.'

The voice that answered fitted the description. 'Are you Mrs Svendsen – Elisabeth Doreen Svendsen? Are you sitting down – because you have been left a legacy – of 204 donkeys!' The shock was immense and worse was to come, as he told me there were debts of £8,500, and any donkeys I could not take would have to be shot as there was no food for the morning!

Of course I had no choice, and so my life changed –
from then to today I have taken in over 12,500
donkeys, set up a world-wide project to try to reach
as many of the 56 million donkeys in the world as
possible, and I started the Elisabeth Svendsen Trust
which helps special needs children in major cities in the
UK using donkeys to bring pleasure, delight and new
skills to their often difficult lives. The trust also visits
old peoples homes and hospices. A lovely surprise
to find a donkey in your bedroom! The full story can
be found in the autobiographies of the first 35 years
(*Down Among the Donkeys* and *For the Love of Donkeys*),
and further on in this book.

I assure you that I could never have achieved all this
without the loyalty and help of my staff – many of

whom have been with me for well over 20 years, and in particular, Paul, my son, who has been my rock! He started helping following that eventful phone call, camping out to protect the Miss Philpin donkeys during his holidays until we were able to organise the fleet of lorries needed to bring them home. All the family helped in the early days, but Paul rejoined the charity after a spell in the RAF, and worked his way up, doing the most menial tasks and eventually becoming Farm Manager of Town Barton Farm – one of our 10 farms.

Some years later, and with growing experience of the Sanctuary's work, he was seconded to Ireland to help set up our sanctuary there and then to Mexico, working with and guiding our teams. Later he came back to Main Office in the UK, organising fund raising and controlling the rapidly expanding computer system. He then joined the executive team, and for the last few years, he has had the job of European Director, setting up much needed sanctuaries in Europe, with projects in Spain and Italy now up and running.

At the age of 21 Paul had written a poem; I loved it and felt it showed his feelings on life and his caring, thoughtful and loving nature.

Thoughts on Life
The leaves are blown
By an unruly wind,
Soon to be cast down
Upon the hard unyielding earth
And blown across barren wastes
That were once beautiful forests.
In time those leaves are absorbed
By that barren soil
And feed and nourish a new
And ever-growing forest
If you compare our lives
With those of the leaves,
You will find that many of us
Although blown by a similar wind
Never try to feed or nourish any
But ourselves.
I hope in a world of hate and anger
Enough leaves will be left
To build a new forest.

Paul Andrew Svendsen
April 1978

Perhaps this inspired me to write poems, sometimes from the donkey's point of view, sometimes from the visitor's point of view. So many people have written asking if they could use the poems in church magazines or in animal welfare information, that I have been persuaded to publish them in a book.

I hope you take time to read these, as they express some of the feelings I share not only with humble donkeys, but also with many friends and supporters.

Worry

It's cold and dark, and I'm standing alone
On a wet, boggy pasture I have to call home
If I try to lie down, my coat gets all wet
And although I am freezing, I'm covered in sweat.

I'm worried

I'm not sure why, but I've pain in my feet
I've turned right around so my back's to the sleet
But my legs are all shaky and I just cannot stand
And sink to the ground, to lie on the land.

I'm frightened

I'm scared that I won't be alive for the dawn
I'm starving, with no chance to eat till the morn
And sleep seems impossible, I'm so very cold
I'm not very big, and I don't think I am old.

I'm shivering

I think I am dreaming – I see a bright light
And I hear people's voices, coming near in the night
'He must be near here – it's where he was seen'
And the footsteps come nearer – I'm lit up with a beam.

I'm startled

'Oh, my God, here he is, in a terrible state
I just hope we've found him before it's too late.'
And gentle hands lift me, I just cannot stand
And they carry me off over wet, boggy land.

And I'm worried again

I cannot remember the rest of the night
I rested on straw as we drove until light
Then tender hands lifted me out of the van
And a kind voice said 'Try to stand if you can.'

And I tried

I was helped to a stable, so warm and so clean
Given hay and water – the best meal I've seen
And they bathed my feet and I felt this was heaven
For God had found me sanctuary in Devon.
And I never had to worry again!

Sad Tales

Of all the donkeys taken in
Many old, and tired and thin
There are some whose stories
  break your heart
It's hard to know quite where to
  start

Mozart, locked up and all alone
His owner is dead, he had no
  home
When rescued, then so full of fear
We had to crawl to get anywhere
  near

And Blackie, expendable in a
  Spanish town
Tortured for pleasure, and then
  forced down
While drunken youths jumped on
  his form
We saved him, brought him back,
  exhausted and torn

Three little colts, all four months
  old
In a strange market place, their
  mothers sold
Alone and scared and full of
  terror
Surely this treatment must be an
  error?

Those of us gathered here today
Are giving our time to remember
  and pray
For family or friends no longer
  able
To talk to the donkeys, to visit
  their stable

To bring them to a happy life
An end to all their toil and strife

And for this, we give thanks.

Getting Old

I'm getting old and soon get tired
And I really can't hear as I could
The winters seem cold
As I keep getting older
And my bones are as stiff as old wood

I had lots of friends and
  it's sad for me
When they get ill and
  finally die
Leaving me on my own
Although it is such a
  lovely home
But with only
  strangers to see

My teeth are all going – they seem to go faster
So food is a problem for me
I don't sleep too well
And my legs tend to swell
And getting up is quite a disaster

But I mustn't complain, I'm doing quite well
And I get what I can from each day
It's so peaceful at night
As I lost my sight
But when dawn comes, I always can tell

With strong, loving arms, when my legs are all wonky
They lift me, and give me a meal
They love me, you see
They really care for me
Because, friends, I'm just an old donkey!

A tired old donkey.

A Donkey's Life

We've had our sad and weary days
As we've stumbled along the lane
We've felt a stick across our back
Overburdened and often in pain

For countless hours on the scorching sand
We've carried our precious loads
For many years we've had no rest
Forced on by stick and goads

When winter came, with the snow and the rain
We've shivered in the cold
No warmth, no feed awarded us
Our bones ached as we grew old

But oh! One blessed glorious day
He looked down on us from above
Our wounds and sores were clear to see
He knew we needed love

And so today we've found our rest
We've found our donkey heaven
We're fed and loved in peaceful quiet
In this wonderful corner of Devon

Reflections

I've woken up and I don't feel well
Dizzy – my head starts to ache,
If only I could stay in bed for a spell
But I must get up for her sake

She's much worse than me, arthritis again,
And I think she's starting a cold
She's finding it hard, putting up with the pain
I suppose it's because we're so old

It's lovely outside and the air's very still
We've been told exercise does us good
Perhaps we can drive to the top of the hill
And then take a walk through the wood

But she definitely knows what she wants to see
It's the donkeys now happy and safe
I wonder if they too get mornings like me
And worry they'll lose this safe place

And go back to life in the bad old days
When each day brought hardship and pain
And cruelty meted in all sorts of ways
Abandoned in cold and in rain

I often wonder when I feel bad
If it's punishment for an earlier wrong?
I was really quite naughty when I was a lad
But never too naughty for long!

But as we walk quietly and reach through the fence
And touch those amazing long ears
It's God's creation itself, that gives life its sense
And with him we forget all our fears.

A Ray of Sunshine

Winter's gone, the cold and frost
Giving way to the sun, I thought was lost
As I stand by the bank, awaiting dawn
Did you know, that like you, donkeys can yawn?

It's been a long night, my ears were so cold
I can't lie down ' cause I'm getting too old
I struggle and roll to get back on my feet
So I've had to stand here all night to sleep.

I have a warm feel now on my back
The hedge stops the wind – I've avoided the gap
And it's creeping along – the sun getting stronger
And, thank God, I'm just not cold any longer.

I'm frightened to think of another cold year
The summer goes fast, and I start to fear
The future, I'm getting so very old
I'm not sure I can stand the frost, and the cold.

But who are these strangers, coming so near?
And talking so quietly, saying 'Come along dear'
And they're leading me out to a big blue van
And I'm helped aboard by a very kind man.

Now the winter is coming but I don't care
I'm warm and I'm fed and walking on air
My feet have been treated, I feel so well
The Sanctuary has saved me from a winter of hell!

2
1982 Donkey Week and Memorial Day

B uilding up the Sanctuary put great pressure on our marriage, and in 1982 Niels left me.

Losing Niels affected not only me, but, also, of course, the children. They were all deeply upset – Lise came over from Denmark to stay with me for a comforting while and the others were so helpful and understanding.

Niels and I had purchased a lovely flat in Torquay, overlooking the sea, with its own private lift to the Penthouse. We had spent over a year designing furniture for every room, and when we were able, spent really happy weekends there, both sailing our small yachts in various races including, in fact, the National 505 championships! Sailing was our main hobby apart from my donkeys. With Niels gone, and all our assets to be split, the flat had to be sold, along with all the furniture.

It was heartbreaking going down to Torquay for the weekend whilst furniture lorries collected some items for home and some to be sold. I had booked into a hotel and it seemed strange to be sitting alone having dinner in the big dining room. There looked to be lots of single people sitting alone at tables and later having coffee in the large lounge. It was a miserable stay – no one seemed to talk to anyone else and most of them sat gazing out at the sea, wrapped in their own thoughts. It did seem a shame – I thought

many of them probably lived in big cities, possibly in the Midlands or the North, and had saved up all year for their holiday in Torquay. Now, once again, they were alone, and unable to make conversation as they probably felt shy.

As I sipped my coffee, it came to me that many of our Donkey Sanctuary subscribers had written to me saying they would love to visit the Sanctuary, but as they were alone they were unable to arrange a trip to see us.

I suddenly thought how nice if we could invite them to the Sanctuary for a week, helping them with their luggage at the train and bus stations; arranging coaches to meet them and take them to the hotels we had booked them into.

We could arrange a visit to our different farms each

day and they would be able to make friends with like minded people – with the donkeys to love and groom. And that was how Donkey Week was born. Our first week was held in May. I don't think in my wildest dreams I had ever thought that it could be such a success! With Julie, Mal and Di Murray, who had recently joined our secretarial team, we planned everything. Everybody arriving at Exeter, either at the railway or coach station, was met by our staff and helped with their luggage to the coaches which then took them to the hotels. I had visited almost every hotel in Sidmouth, and instead of asking for a discount for our visitors, I had suggested that they treated each person as an individual and charged the rate they normally charged, but each hotel gave us 10% of the accommodation proceeds for The Donkey Sanctuary. Eight hotels had been very happy to join the scheme and to have visitors at a time when Sidmouth is normally very quiet. Julie and Di liaised with our supporters in making the arrangements and Di became almost a full-time Donkey Week organizer as everybody's worries or problems regarding the week landed on her desk. The first morning when the coaches arrived at the Sanctuary I managed to get on each coach and explained to everybody what we did, what we hoped to achieve, and what we would try to do for them during the week, and as they got off the coaches all my willing staff took over. It was apparent that there was an enormous rapport between the visitors and the donkeys and, indeed, between the visitors and the staff, all of whom really appreciated the change from routine work to looking after the visitors

29

and travelling round different farms. The donkeys loved every single minute of the week; so many people loved them, petted them and some just wanted to stand and groom the donkeys for the week. It was a time of deep satisfaction for all those involved. About 110 people attended that first Donkey Week.

The first day we spent at the Sanctuary, and then on the second day everybody got on the coaches and went out to Town Barton Farm. Here Paul had laid on rides on the tractors around the farm to show everybody the extent of the property and to see the donkeys in even the furthest quarters of the farm. Each day another farm entertained our visitors and each evening I went down to Sidmouth and had dinner at a different hotel so that I could see the guests and make sure that everybody was perfectly happy!

We not only arranged Donkey Week the next year – we have done it for 25 years now, and average over 400 visitors every year!

When Donkey Weekers have attended for 10 years, they get a special red Sanctuary shirt, which they wear with deep pride, and they take on the job of looking after the novice Donkey Weekers!

Everyone loves the visits to the farms, some just content to groom and stroke the donkeys in the barns; others enjoy walking with their favourite donkey along the beautiful Devon and Dorset landscape. Over the years I have become known as the Mother of the Donkeys and this has expanded to being 'Mother' to all the Donkey Weekers. The really golden oldies particularly

love calling me 'Mother', having lost their own, but it
must seem strange to non Donkey Weekers to hear me
chatting to an obvious O.A.P. and her referring to me as
Mother!

We knew that many people would love to enjoy
a donkey orientated church service on Sunday. I
had been a member of Salcombe Regis choir so I
approached the vicar to see if he would organise a
service for our special week. He did, and it was really
appreciated. Unfortunately (or perhaps fortunately
for us as it turned out) he was appointed to another
church outside the parish and I asked him if he could
recommend another vicar and his recommendation was
Peter Leverton. I made a telephone call to him and we
agreed to meet! What a lovely man! I knew we had

found a treasure as he loves all the things the Sanctuary
stands for – a deep love of animals and people, and
the more he found out about us, the more he became
involved. He gave a beautiful service at his first meeting
of our Donkey Weeks, and has become 'our vicar'.

Originally the services were held in our marquee but
of course a church would be much better. We were
delighted when the village church in Tedburn St Mary
offered to have us. The church is practically within the
boundary of our Sanctuary farm there – home to over
400 donkeys!

The parishioners have been marvellous in providing
lunch on the day of our visit, and placing chairs up the
aisle to accommodate our 400 Donkey Weekers. A
collection is taken during the service – the first time
to help fund a new roof! It is wonderful to see the
church absolutely packed, and to hear the donkeys

joining in with the hymns! Some of my poems relate to these occasions – I was asked to write a poem for each Donkey Week and was particularly inspired by the service at Tedburn.

Donkey Week always ends with a talk from Mother, and I'm afraid, frequently naughty stories! One of my favourites is this one –

An elderly man goes to visit his doctor. 'I've not come about me,' he says, 'It's the wife – she's very deaf, but she won't accept it and won't come to you to discuss it.'

The doctor ponders and says, 'If you do a little test for me it will help greatly. I will be able to gauge the level of her deafness, and when she comes for her flu jab I will arrange to see her. Make sure she is not facing you, and try her with a question from a long way away, about 30 feet, and if she doesn't answer go 5 feet nearer and try again until she hears you and let me know the distance.'

The husband goes home. As luck would have it, his wife has her back to him and is peeling potatoes at the sink. Standing outside the door, he asks in a normal voice, 'What's for dinner, darling?' No reply. He steps forward 5 feet and asks again, 'What's for dinner darling?' Again no reply. He is now only 2 feet away. 'What's for dinner darling?' His wife turns round and says, 'For the third time – CHICKEN.'

Some of the nicest letters we get following Donkey Week are from single people who have made a lasting friendship. I particularly remember two middle-aged

men, both single and from Wales. Ivan wrote after returning home, 'I can't believe the friend I met at Donkey Week – do you know Len lives in the same town, and every Sunday we have sat alone to have Sunday lunch – now we have met we shall have lunch together every week.'

Also a lovely letter from Sylvia Horne:

Dear Mrs S,

This is my 5th Donkey Week. When I came to the first, it was partly out of curiosity to see the place in which our 2 'rehab' donkeys had spent part of their life; partly to discover more about donkeys in general. As we had no one to care for our animals while we were away, my husband stayed at home to look after them.

It was clear from the newsletter that many people enjoyed D.W. but I rather wondered ... However, it was only a week and I remember saying that even if it was really dreadful I could surely stand it for so short a time!

Of course I loved every minute and at the end of the week, I joined the Torbay hotel 'regulars' as they booked their rooms for the following year. Like so many people, I've had a lot of sadness and stress since then and really wonder how I would manage without D.W. to look forward to.

In addition to enjoying the happiness at the Sanctuary, meeting the lovely donkeys, and chatting to the staff, I have made many friends among 'us visitors' and I am lucky that some live near enough to visit us – although I suspect that they mainly come to feed carrots to the donkeys.

Normally Donkey Week Sunday luncheon ends after various speeches, but one year our visitors had a surprise for us. They had decided to have a special ten-year celebration and, to the Sanctuary staff's amazement, two little figures appeared in beautiful donkey costumes and presented the most amusing and clever stage show to the music of 'The Stripper'. The two little donkeys came to the top table and led me onto the stage, and to the rapturous applause of everybody I was able to take off their 'heads' to reveal Mo Flenley and Sylvia Horne!

Many of our Donkey Weekers also visit for Memorial Day – they love not only the service but the blessing of our lovely memorials on our 7 miles of walks.

I've been long aware of the value of legacies in our work – from the earliest day careful records have been kept and every person is remembered on Memorial Day. Many people have purchased a bench, or a tree, in memory of a loved one or sometimes a pet. Each memorial is decorated with a reed cross on the first Saturday in October, the nearest date to the Feast Day of St Francis of Assisi, a lover of animals.

We dedicate a Vicarmobile for the day and with Peter, the vicar, we visit the families standing by their particular bench or tree, covered by flowers – all very moving.

As the Vicarmobile drives round the walk, the high

hedge prevents those ploughing the adjoining field from seeing the vehicle, and stories of a 'floating vicar' cause us some amusement.

Once again, during the service, one of the executives, Richard Barnes, reads a poem I have written for the occasion – his beautiful expressive voice as he reads, plus the words, cause many tears amongst our audience, of 500. But this is what the day is about – remembering loved ones who loved donkeys and who will always be remembered.

The donkeys actually attend the service, walking down the centre aisle and standing in pride of place – and they have been known to join in the hymns!

I do hope you enjoy the lovely watercolours and the following poems:

Donkey Week

Each year it comes at the start of May
When each day of the week is Donkey Day
For a loyal group we all hold dear
Who come and support us every year

Each one a friend, a well known face
Perhaps now walking at slower pace
But oh, so welcome, old and new
Swelling the ranks of the favoured few

Who recognise the good Lord's hand
In creating the Donkey we understand
This gentle creature trusted to us
From a life of toil, borne without fuss

In seven days our world was created
Today's our chance, with our work abated
On Sunday, on this religious day
To take a moment to stop and pray

To pray for donkeys here in Devon
That this may be their Donkey Heaven
And that when May comes round next year
Each one of us will be sitting here.

Let us Pray

Let us kneel, and let us pray,
Here in this wonderful Church today
Pray for all animals in our care
Especially for donkeys, no matter where
As they toil in their endless tasks

Pray for their owners in conditions so bleak
Tired and desperate, with no food to eat
In far off lands, many parched with no rain
Where donkeys stand waiting to carry the grain
Which has withered and died with the grass

Pray for the donkey covered with sores
Patiently working at unceasing chores
Carrying bricks, and water, and sand
Until his legs buckle – he can't understand
Why he cannot get up from the ground

Pray that our help can reach out to him
That gentle hands touch his body, so thin
And sweet healing ointment is put on his back
And his owner is helped with the gift of the sack
To protect his bleeding, aching body

Please hear our prayer, for life can be hell
For the donkey, his owner and children as well
And I'm sure were you here on earth with us all
As you looked to his suffering, you would recall
The day he carried you in triumph

Donkey Service in Tedburn Church

Today's a very special day
In Tedburn's Church we've come to pray
Surrounded by Donkeys, large and small
We Donkey Weekers love them all

We've seen them come, afraid and thin
No matter how many, all let in
To find a place of peace and rest
And all the things they love best

From years of neglect, years of pain
They struggle in, some drenched with rain
Cold, unloved, beaten by man
This surely can't be in God's plan?

But help has come, and here at last
Their problems now are in the past
We know their likes, and know their fears
And they'll be safe for donkeys' years!

So as we sing and as we pray
We give our thanks to God today
For humble donkeys large and small
For we love them, one and all !

Tedburn Church.

Remembering

The walks are ready, the donkeys fine
It's Memorial Day for another time
So many, many people here,
Remembering those so very dear
No longer with us, left us all
But with lovely memories to recall

At peace at last from fear and pain
How we wish we could see them once again
Just to hug and hold their hand
But they're all gone to the Promised Land

Some miss a dog, a special friend
Brave and loyal to the very end
And what a hole in our lives they leave
But now we are here with time to grieve

And some a partner, mum or dad
A child – it makes us all feel very sad
We feel that God from up on high
Has let us down – we can only sigh

We can't forget them and on this day
It gives us time to think and pray
To know that here, they are at rest
Never forgotten and specially blessed.

Remembering.

Friends for life.

Making the World much Better

I'm asking a question here today
Do you believe there is a way,
That we, each one, can make a change
Some cruel things can re-arrange

To make our lives much better?

Do you believe we have a chance
Each one of us, to give a glance
At things we see and do not like
Be brave enough to stand and fight

To make our world much better?

Each one of us has lost a friend
A loved one on whom we could depend
It could be husband, pet or wife
Left us for another life

We pray their world is better

Let's quietly pray for those we mourn
They'll never see another dawn
Remembering all their little ways
And all those wonderful happy days

Which make our world much better

But here's a chance to make your mark
Stand up for those who bray and bark
Defend those with no voice to speak
Protect our animals, the poor and weak

To make their world much better

For the Love of Donkeys

As we gather here today
It's to take part in our special Memorial Day
We've come to Sidmouth from far and wide
To remember the loved ones we've lost – with pride.

Maybe it's a partner, child, animal or friend
Such sadness for us when their lives had to end
But they won't be forgotten, we'll always recall
The joy and the love that they gave to us all.

There's one special thing binding us together
That makes us come here, whatever the weather
It's a feeling for donkeys that everyone loved
Not just those here, but those from above.

The humblest of creatures, with deep knowing eyes
What thoughts do they have when their friend dies?
We know that they miss them, they grieve just like us
But they have to get on with their lives with no fuss.

And so here today, we'll stand up and sing
Encouraged to make even the rafters ring
Because go on we must, and make people aware
That comfort can come from the simplest prayer.

A Place of Dreams

Something made me come today
I couldn't let anything stand in my way
I've had a bad cough, and a pain in my head
Which meant I spent most of last week laying in bed
The family told me to stay well away
They said it would upset me, they all had their say
But I had to come.

It's the sort of place that makes me feel
That the dreams I have of life are real
That there really can be a place of calm
To relax and unwind, where none come to harm
From the humble donkeys at rest in the fields
To the little dog at its master's heels
As they visit their tree on the walk.

I remember so well, in those days long gone by
When we would walk slowly together, he and I
Admiring the benches, the plaques on the wall
The tree we had planted, now grown so tall
And I know that today, as I stand by our tree
That he is in Heaven, looking down on me
As our lovely memorial is blessed.

God's Wonderful Plan

The summer's gone, and autumn's here
Memorial Day, and another year
Where does time go, and what have we done
That will leave a mark in the years to come?

Each one here knows of wasted time
Of day passing day without a sign
That we've wasted and squandered another chance
To help someone needy, passed by without glance.

It seemed so easy years ago
Life seemed for ever, growing old so slow
But now – what a shock! Time has taken its toll
And we must face the future and set a new goal.

Those we have come to remember today
Loved poor little donkeys and showed us the way
That we too could help, by giving our love
To people and animals – helped from above.

For what can we do for animals and man
Must all be a part of God's wonderful plan
And because of our presence right here and now
Let's all pray together and make a new vow

To treasure each moment we have one another
To help where we're needed without any bother
And for this Sanctuary daily to pray
For help for the donkeys here every day.

Missing you.

Missing You
The summer is going and winter draws near
I wonder what life's like for you, my dear
If only I could just reach out to you
And just for a moment, to hold your hand
But you've gone, slipped away, like the last grain of sand.

Where will you be, as I lie alone in our bed
Will the cold wind bring the coldness I dread
If only I could just reach out to you
And feel you next to me, close and warm
No need to fear the winds and the storm.

I'm here, with friends, near the donkeys we love
All remembering those looking down from above
If only I could just reach out to you
And together we would walk to our peaceful seat
And sit, watching the donkeys — our favourite treat.

Do they know more than us — do they miss their friends
As we miss each other when our life ends?
If only I could reach out to you
I'd say goodbye for the very last time
And feel your soft lips as they kissed mine.

3
The Slade Centre and The Elisabeth Svendsen Trust for Children and Donkeys

Because of my special interest in children, and my love of donkeys, I thought how wonderful it would be if I could put these two loves together and so in 1975 I decided to see for myself what the reaction between the two would be!

I rang George Hopkins, the head of the local school for children with special needs at Honiton, Mill Water School, and mentioned my idea of letting the children have the opportunity to love, cuddle and ride some of our donkeys. I rather thought he would ridicule the

suggestion, but he was immediately enthusiastic and thought just the experience of meeting large gentle animals could be of help, even to the most mentally and physically disabled children.

Within a week, he arrived with a group of eight children, one in a wheelchair, some hyperactive, some autistic and some really physically disabled. We had put eight donkeys in a small barn and gradually put them all together. The results were amazing! The hyperactive children quietened as the donkey nuzzled them. The autistic children were obviously moved and the child in the wheelchair shouted with joy as a donkey put its head on her lap to enjoy having his ears stroked.

From the donkeys' point of view, it was equally successful. They seemed to know the children were special, and even though sometimes their skin was pinched and pulled, they stood stoically, even enjoying the contact.

We tried a few children riding the donkeys with even better results, and George and I looked at each other and knew it was a very special moment.

We almost immediately started putting together a mobile unit, and within 12 months were visiting almost every special needs' school in our area. Westland Helicopters made us a special lightweight cart. This had a ramp for wheelchairs, and was light enough for a donkey to pull, so even those children over the 8-stone riding weight restriction could enjoy a ride in the cart.

We formed a charity and began the long battle to

build a special indoor centre where we could bring the children to enjoy riding all the year round. Obviously, for the donkeys' sakes, we could not travel to the schools in the winter – so the children could not make the progress needed with such a long break. A good example of this was a little boy of seven with serious physical problems with his legs, a type of scissor leg. When he first started riding, because his joints would not allow his legs to separate, he had to ride almost on the neck of the donkey; gradually each week the exercise and movement meant he could sit a little further back, and by autumn he was almost able to sit on the saddle. By the time spring came, however, with no riding for months, when he had his first ride, it was back nearly to the donkey's neck!

Other children, too, made gains in agility, balance and

motivation and we all knew that a year-round centre was a must!

What a battle, though! We had every possible reason for rejection thrown at us – from the local council, East Devon District Council, planning authorities, all seemed against us. Our Patrons, Trustees and all the special needs' schools wrote in our favour, and eventually, after three years of effort, The Slade Centre was built and at last my dream was coming true.

It was to be some years before we could expand and open another centre in Birmingham. Our original charity, The Slade Centre, restricted us to working in the local area, so a new charity had to be formed, The Elisabeth Svendsen Trust for Children and Donkeys, to allow for national expansion.

Like Topsy, the dream grew. The success of Birmingham was amazing. Inner city children had fewer opportunities of relating to donkeys than had those in our local area, and being able to see and stroke the gentle donkeys and, even better, ride them was a turning point in the lives of many children. The help of Birmingham City Council in allowing us to rent land in their beautiful Sutton Park, and the co-operation and encouragement of the friends of Sutton Park played a big part in its success. I had also been involved in the Queensway Trust in Birmingham where they had been running a scheme funded by the Government involving donkeys. When the government funding stopped, the Trust closed down. Sue Brennan, a qualified AI (BHS Advanced Instructor) had been working for them, and

Sue became our principal of the newly built centre.

I'll never forget the first day the children came to the centre. The playroom was laid out with new toys, the arena was big, warm and brightly lit, and there were donkeys waiting for them. The first two children in were from different ethnic backgrounds – both aged about five, one a golden-haired, blue-eyed little girl, the other, a dark, black-haired little boy – and were holding hands. They stopped at the door, looking at the play area and toys, then glanced towards the arena, and the donkeys, and, with a great shout of joy, ran together to the welcoming donkeys!

Raising funds for this charity has never been easy – many elderly people feel they may have paid all their lives to support schooling and don't feel they need to pay now. Some feel it's the Government's job, but we feel that something as lovely and rewarding as this for these children with such terrible disadvantages is more than worthwhile and we will continue to expand EST in the future!

We now have centres in Leeds, Manchester, Birmingham, Sidmouth and Plymouth, and hope shortly to open another – Northern Ireland being the favourite venue. We never make any charge to schools or children – all is provided free.

Our centres now have expanded their work to take donkeys to visit schools, hospices and old people's homes in their areas.

Local schools welcome the chance to let their pupils

learn about animal welfare, and in particular donkeys' needs. Some schools are able to visit an Elisabeth Svendsen Trust centre near them, where the children can meet other children less fortunate than themselves.

I have always tried to help older people as well, and am constantly appalled that these elderly citizens can be left, sitting day after day, sunk down in their chairs, with apparently nothing to do but stare at the carpet. Many stay in their rooms all day with no incentive to do anything. The visit of a real live donkey in their lounge certainly makes them sit up and take interest! The donkeys love the fuss and attention as they visit each person, receiving a cuddle, and bringing a spark of life to the elderly recipient. In one case two elderly sisters had been in a home for two years and had never been downstairs, living together amongst the few private possessions they had been allowed to bring, and their memories.

One day that changed – the door opened and in came – a donkey! They were overwhelmed and got out of their beds to cuddle and stroke him! The donkeys are amazing, not only going up flights of stairs, but even using the lift if big enough!

As the donkeys left that day the staff saw the two ladies watching through the window and called up to them, 'We'll be here next Wednesday.' The staff at the home noticed an immediate difference. They were asked ten times a day, 'Is it Wednesday yet?' and when Wednesday came, for the first time for months, the sisters were dressed.

As the donkey lorry arrived, the staff looked up at the window and waved. As the two donkeys came out of the lorry, two little old ladies literally tottered down the steps and each headed for a donkey. They were helped to walk the donkey on to the grass lawn and from that day they started to come downstairs and talk to the other residents – a breakthrough. The poem Donkeys' Years is based on true fact!

Donkeys' Years

What's the point of getting up
Of living through another day
The same as the last
In a long, long line
A waste, I say.

I've been put here to wait to die
My home has gone and the money used
To fund this place – no good to cry
No future now I'm 95
They say I'm lucky to be alive

Alive! A joke! There's no hope here
My pets all gone — and the days so
  long
Each one the same, from dawn to
  dusk
Just memories now, and they're not
  strong
And I hope the end is near.

I can hear a noise outside my room
And the door is pushed open as I sit
  up
And I can't believe what I can see
There's a donkey coming up to me
The last time I saw one was by the sea!

My hands reach out to touch his muzzle,
So soft and moist — he loves my cuddle
And he puts his head right into my bed
And my tears drop down on the
Top of his head
As we slowly rock together.

I just can't bear to see him go
So quiet and gentle — he seems to know
The need I have to see him soon
Just to have him here, in my room
Has made my life worth living.

They've got me a book full of donkey tales
And it's made me laugh, despite my ails
And I can't wait for lunch,
Because soon after noon
He's coming again, and despite all my fears
They've promised he's coming for
  donkeys' years!

The Ride

I just can't move my arms and leg
I really don't know why.
My Mum keeps saying 'please stand up'
And I do my best to try.

The days seem long, and I get tired
Lying on a bed all day
'If only something nice could happen'
I close my eyes and pray.

For seven long years I've been like this
Though my mind is really clear.
I can't understand why my legs won't work
And the adults say, 'Never mind dear.'

But something happened yesterday
That has brought some hope to me
They lifted me into the family car
And they drove to a place near the sea.

And they wheeled my bed through a great big door
And they gave me a terrible fright.
Because in came an animal, oh so big
Who stood by me, and blocked out the light.

He put down his head and touched my hand
His breath was all warm and wet.
I could feel his soft hair brushing my arm
It was a feeling I'd come to forget.

And I longed to reach out and touch the long ears
And I longed to get out of my bed.
It was joy that I felt, as they lifted me up
And then put a hard hat on my head.

And then, oh the thrill, I was up on his back
Looking down on my Mum and my Dad.
But why was she crying, and holding my hand
When I was feeling so glad?

The tingle I felt in my arm had come back –
I could feel a strange buzz in my feet.
And I tried and I tried to sit up straight
On my wonderful donkey so sweet.

But then it was over and back on the ground
They held me as close as they could.
For I longed and I prayed to touch his soft nose
And my hands knew that they really should.

And he nuzzled my hand, and my fingers uncurled
And my arm moved the very first time.
And my tears wet his face as I knew that at last
With his help, God had given a sign.

The Autistic Child

The first thing I remembered, when I was so small
Was the colour of my mother's dress, same shade as the wall,
A beautiful green, that I loved to see
And I remember touching it as I sat on her knee

She rocked and she cuddled me every day
But I couldn't find any words to say.
My sister, she shouted, and spoke in my face
I could hear her alright, but just stared into space.

If I tried to make words, they all seemed to slide
And my head felt all dizzy, I felt sick inside
And my mother kept crying, it made me feel sad
And I longed to say something, to make her feel glad

But as I grew older, I still couldn't speak
And I worried and worried and just couldn't eat.
The days seemed to drag and I grew very weak
My mother asked God if he'd help me to speak

The way that he answered he told her in prayer
And she listened, and arranged for me to go there.
To a very special place in rural East Devon
Where donkeys and children feel they've found heaven

And there I met something which I've never seen,
A lady, all dressed in my favourite green,
Let me into a stall – put my hand out in space
And suddenly felt this enormous soft face,
It was all warm and furry, and breathed on my hand
And as I felt further it moved in the sand
And they lifted me up and my mind became clear
As I rode that dear Donkey – my father was near

Then a strange thing happened – I heard a new sound.
It was me! I was shouting – I looked around
And my father was crying as I shouted in glee
Said my very first word, and it was 'Donkee'!

Based on a true story.

4
Overseas

I was well aware that the problems facing donkeys in the UK were only tiny, compared to the millions of donkeys working overseas. A holiday visit to Tunisia in 1972 had allowed me to see for myself the terrible conditions the small, starved donkeys were in. Young, thin and starving, they were forced to carry adults often weighing more than themselves, or to drag large heavy clumsy carts, loaded with people, with harnesses made up of wire and wood. My heart went out to them, and I was determined our help must reach out to the developing countries. Once again I decided to set up a charity, and on 21 January 1976, the first meeting of the International Donkey Protection Trust was called, with funds of £250!

It seems amazing that from that small start the charity has grown, is now amalgamated with the Donkey Sanctuary, and has projects in 15 countries with major work in Mexico, Ethiopia, Kenya, Egypt and India. There are over 56 million donkeys out there, all struggling to help their impoverished owners by taking and fetching goods to market and carrying water.

Starting projects in other countries is never without its problems. Each country has separate laws and religions, many of which impact on our work; and I certainly met some problems trying to promote donkey welfare in countries where the plight of their human owners was nearly as bad as the plight of the donkeys!

However, it soon became clear that one of the biggest problems I was facing was that of the early demise of the overworked donkeys.

In the UK, I knew the donkey's average life span was around 27 years, and some could live to over 50 – so why were the donkeys, so desperately needed, dying around 11 years old? Of course, they had little food and were terribly overworked and suffered dreadful wounds from ill fitting harnesses, but was this causing them early death? I rather suspected it could be caused by parasites, worms in the gut, which shared what little food the donkey was given. These parasites eventually weakened the gut to such an extent that it ruptured and an embolism killed the donkey. To test my theory my friend, June, and I travelled to remote corners of Africa, collecting dung, and checked the contents with our microscopes! It seemed the theory was right – the samples teemed with every known parasite, and the veterinary profession was helpful in endorsing our findings!

It was this discovery that got us working in Lamu – a small island off the Kenyan coast. I was visiting Nairobi to meet the KSPCA and open a new barn we had funded for them, when a story blew up about the donkeys in Lamu having to wear nappies as they were polluting the narrow streets of the town! I decided to take a trip to see how many donkeys were there and what condition they were in, so took the tiny plane down to Lamu.

The guide who met me, called Abdalla, was determined I should know the full history of the island and visit the museum and other items of historical interest. I was equally determined just to see as many donkeys as possible! Eventually I won and we ended up with Abdalla taking me to his uncle's shamba, where about twelve donkeys were kept! They were in appalling condition. Two at least had tetanus and were in a state of collapse, and one had been attacked by a hyena and had a terrible open gash on its quarters. I had my donkey first aid bag with me and was able to stitch the terrible wound closed, but of course I had none of the desperately needed antibiotics and was really worried about the results of my work. Apparently there were no vets on the island.

On my return to Nairobi, I sent for Bill Jordan, one of our Trustees and a vet, and asked if he would come out and accompany me to Lamu. Bless him, Bill arrived the next day. He also brought a supply of anthelmintic (worm paste). We set off immediately for Lamu, to be met again by Abdalla – this time only too keen to take us to the donkeys. Bill was complimentary about my handiwork and was able to give the much needed shot of antibiotic. We explained to Abdalla about the need to worm the thin and emaciated donkeys on the island and he arranged for us to dose the donkeys of his uncle and other relatives, and broadcast in the town a free clinic would be held in the morning for free treatment to anyone's donkey!

We were disappointed to find only 4 donkeys waiting for us the following morning, but then a strange thing happened. A young man ran down the main street, holding a piece of newspaper on which rested a handful of donkey dung! 'Doo Doos, Doo Doos,' he was shouting – showing the smelly lumps under the eyes of everyone he could stop – and there, extremely visible to the eye, were crawling worms – revolting bots, the result of the previous day's worming!! The result was amazing – within an hour over fifty donkeys came for treatment, and the lives of the donkeys on Lamu changed for ever.

We have been working on Lamu for over twenty-five years now. Donkeys are the only means of transport there, the streets are so narrow and we have seen such an improvement in the donkeys. We built a lovely clinic there, as donkeys will always be used, not only on Lamu, but on all the other small surrounding islands we visit regularly. Abdalla became our manager and still runs the clinic.

To encourage the islanders to respect and care for the donkeys we hold an annual competition for the best kept stallion, mare and foal, and give good prizes, which are really appreciated by the owners. Great care is

taken to have their donkeys looking really well, and one year I was watching the boys washing the donkeys in the sea, and was surprised to see one donkey having its teeth brushed by a scrubbing brush! The way to age a donkey is by their teeth and when judging I had always looked in the donkey's mouth. They thought I was looking to see if its teeth were clean!

The local children loved to watch the competition – they were very poor on the islands and we always took as many small toys as we could to give them. Often shops let us have small metal cars very cheaply and they were really treasured, often the only toy these children would ever have; and they would keep them and show us year after year. It makes you think when you see how many toys our children get and are often taken for granted.

On one of the islands we visited, Chundwa, Abdalla told me of the fate of a Mama. Her husband had died out fishing, and she was on her own, with no family or children. Almost blind, she spent all day lying on a hard bed, made of dried palm leaves and had to rely on someone in the small impoverished village giving her food and water.

I sat with her a while one day, and left her with a few Kenyan shillings. Abdalla told me later that she was so grateful she cried, and insisted every shilling went to her neighbours to pay for the scraps of food they gave her. Until she died I arranged, privately, for Abdalla to visit and give her a little money every time the team went to Chundwa.

In the majority of cases the hard treatment given to

the donkeys is not done out of cruelty. The owners
are also impoverished and really try to look after their
animals. In Ethiopia if a donkey dies, it can take a year's
salary to replace it, money the family doesn't have. So
giving the donkey a further healthy five years of life can
make a big difference to the community.

We see many sad cases during our work, and we long
to help more people and animals. Some villages are so
remote they never see a doctor and look on us to help
humans as well as animals. Of course, we are not really
allowed to do this, but I was so horrified in one village
in Ethiopia, I just had to do something. They brought
this man on a stretcher. His legs below the knee were
three times the normal size, and covered in suppurating

sores. The only thing I had with me was a jar of green Dermobian – wonderful for treating and healing the ghastly saddle galls we find on donkeys every day! Following his pleading and crying, I gently rubbed the ointment over both his legs, and they carried him away.

At the time we were conducting a trial of anthelmintics in three remote villages outside Debre Zeit. In one village all the donkeys were dosed with an excellent but expensive anthelmintic. In the second a good and cheap anthelmintic was used. In the third village the donkeys were given a placebo – a dose of paste with vitamins but no wormer in.

On the third visit we were met by the head man, who pulled at my arm – 'Come, come,' he said, and took me to a mud hut. Outside was sitting a man with a familiar face. To my horror he stood up and undid his trousers! He stood looking at me, his trousers round his ankles – and I recognised the legs!! Now back to normal size and the skin all dry and flaky where it had peeled. I was given a very embarrassing but enthusiastic hug before the trousers were pulled up! Dermobian had worked again!

The results of the trial were amazing. We were fêted by village one who had fatter and healthier donkeys, thanked by village two with improved donkeys and had to almost run from village three, who felt cheated. We had to promise to return again as their donkeys were still thin!

Our teams around the developing world really do a magnificent job. Mobile clinics are met with relief and delight. It is so rewarding to see the donkeys gradually improve, and begin to get at least a little enjoyment

out of life and to see the locals' pride at their donkeys' well-being.

There is still much to do, however, and the work will certainly not finish in my lifetime!

I feel so happy that my son, Paul, who has worked alongside me for so very many years, is now the Sanctuary's Director for Europe. We continually have problems there, the worst, of course, being at Villanueva de la Vera, where every Shrove Tuesday a donkey is ridden and dragged around the town in a terrible ceremony. He is surrounded by men with guns and sticks, and is pushed to the ground many times. Brandy is poured down his throat and he is crushed and punched. Despite every effort, we have been unable to stop this horrific event; even new laws passed have not prevented this annual horror! On one occasion, after being told that the donkey was going to be killed, and accompanied by the national press, we were able to rescue 'Blackie' who became quite famous and lived the rest of his years happily and safely in the Sanctuary at Sidmouth, with his companion Lola!

Paul still has problems to face in Spain, but he has set up two sanctuaries there as well as one in Italy. As I write this he is in Romania where a group of donkeys purchased to be shipped to Italy for meat were prevented by the authorities from being shipped as the paperwork was incomplete. No longer having a market for the donkeys, they were just turned away to fend for themselves, and Paul found them being fed poisoned corn by the farmers on whose land the donkeys were living. These are now being taken to our new sanctuary

in Italy after being treated by vets.

The work goes on ... and on ... and on! Endless work in developing countries and Europe, and still the problems in the UK.

This little book, and my poems, try to illustrate how important donkeys are to all ages, and all people around the world. I do hope you have enjoyed it. We don't help just donkeys; helping them helps the poorest people in the world – and gives real pleasure to both old and young.

The African Mama

I'm getting old and losing my sight
And it's always hot in my hut at night.
In fact I can't see very much at all
And I have to be careful that I don't fall.

If you close your eyes you'll be like me
Please try now, then I'll have company.
It's amazing how we can shut out light,
Turn a wonderful day into darkest night.

My donkey shows me the way to town
I hold onto her collar, she won't let me down.
I've managed to balance some corn on her back
But I'm not sure I've properly tied on the sack.

Disaster strikes as we walk on the road
I hear the noise as she loses her load.
I try hard to see, but the lorries raise dust
And I'm so very frightened, but find it I must.

I feel a touch, a hand on my back
'Here, let me help you. I'll pick up your sack.
Just move here with me to the side of the road,
I'll help your donkey and refix your load.'

'Your poor donkey's thin and covered in sores
Does she belong to you – is she yours?'
It's the kindest voice I've heard for years
And suddenly my eyes are just filling with tears.

As if in a dream I'm helped in a van
My donkey led in by the very kind man.
He is talking so gently, and giving her feed
And now he is asking me what I need.

A miracle has happened for donkey and me
He's arranged for a doctor to help me to see.
They've lent me a donkey until mine is strong
And they help working donkeys all the day long.

My life began changing from that very day
And now I can see, as I kneel and I pray,
And thank God for the wonderful gift of sight
For seeing the daylight instead of the night.

The Ethiopian Donkey

The mornings are dark, and it's so very cold
When my master appears at the door
My bones are all aching, I'm getting quite old
And it's hard to get up from the floor.

He helps me to rise, puts a cloth on my back
Then it's out in the cold morning air
My load is enormous, heavy grain in the sack
But I wait while he kneels in prayer.

Then the journey begins and we walk to the track
To the market, so many miles away
Where the price for the grain, and amount in the sack
Will either make, or ruin, his day.

The dawn has arisen as we reach the mill
And we take up our place in the queue
Surrounded by donkeys so many are ill
And the humans are thin and sick too.

The pain and the suffering are all plain to see
The donkeys exhausted and starved
As the sacks are unloaded they drop to one knee
So grateful the load has been halved.

But into the yard that is full of despair
Come a small group of people with aid
Their mission to soothe, to treat and repair
Give the donkeys new life – all unpaid.

I feel soothing hands on the galls on my back
And have medicine to make me live longer
And they treat my feet, give me food that I lack
And suddenly I feel a lot stronger.

My master is happy, has had a good day
The grain brought good money at last
And I feel so good as I go on my way
The pain I had felt now all passed.

His family wait as we come down the road
They see food and fuel on my back
They are shouting with joy as they start to unload
Thanking God for the goods that they lack.

And then together they kneel and pray
To give thanks to their Lord up above
And I listen and know that what happened today
Was truly the result of his love.

Why Donkeys

This is a question that I often hear
and I suppose that to me it is so very clear
but to help you find out, from A – Z
I've listed some assets just from my head

There are many to choose from A – D
from Asian History, its use clear to see
and its value with children, who learn from their ride
and gain new achievements they display with great pride

The most economical animal, its cost is so low
that in every poor country they're kept on the go
helping the poorest, their dung provides fuel
and they carry their goods and their children to school

As guard dogs down under they protect the sheep,
from wild dogs and snakes, at the sound of a bleat
They tackle the problem, with kicks and with teeth,
and protect their charges, their lambs safe beneath

In China their main use is producing fine milk
for children, and producing soap, smooth, soft as silk
In Africa it's traction, pulling great carts
with loads so enormous, it just breaks your heart

In war they have proved a great help to man
carrying bombs and sidewinders, is this in God's plan?
But gentle and patient, poor women can use them
abroad where they often work harder than men

To me, he has helped man the most on the earth
so why so derided, abused in his work?

My job is to champion, the donkey my friends
and this I will do, until my life ends.